CHOIR & PRAISE TEAM

SING OF HIS LOVE

ARRANGED BY CAMP KIRKLAND

ALLEGIS
PUBLICATIONS

CONTENTS

I Could Sing of Your Love Forever

with
The Love of Christ

Words and Music by
MARTIN SMITH
Arranged by Camp Kirkland

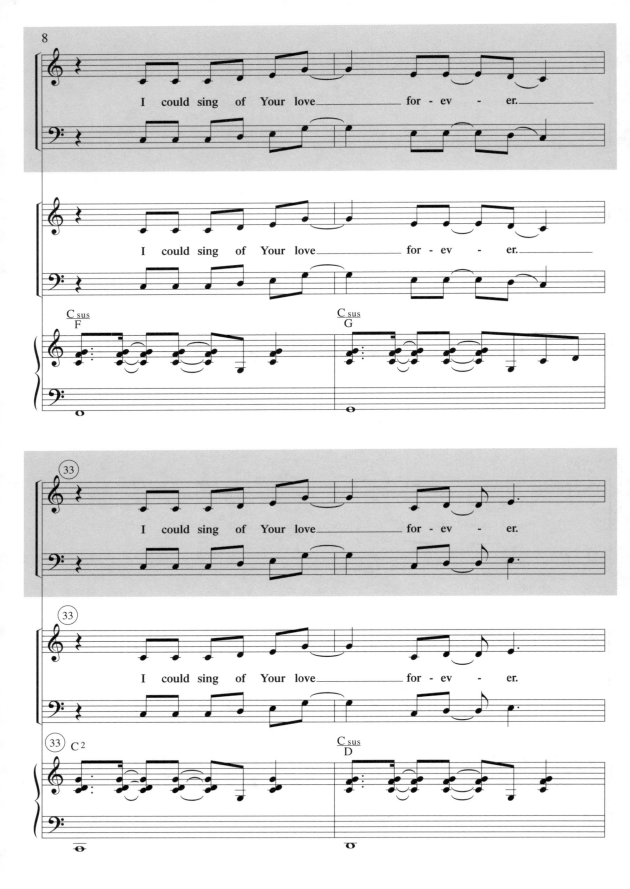

10

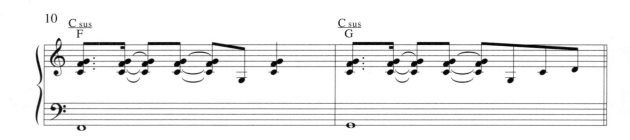

I'm hap-py to be in__ the truth, and I will dai-ly lift__ my hands,

For I will al-ways sing of when Your love came down.__

12

16

CD: 7

I could sing of Your love for - ev - er.

73

I could sing of Your love for - ev - er.

I could sing of Your love_____ for - ev - er._____

I could sing of Your love_____ for - ev - er.

grad. decresc.

grad. decresc.

grad. decresc.

Oo_____

grad. decresc.

19

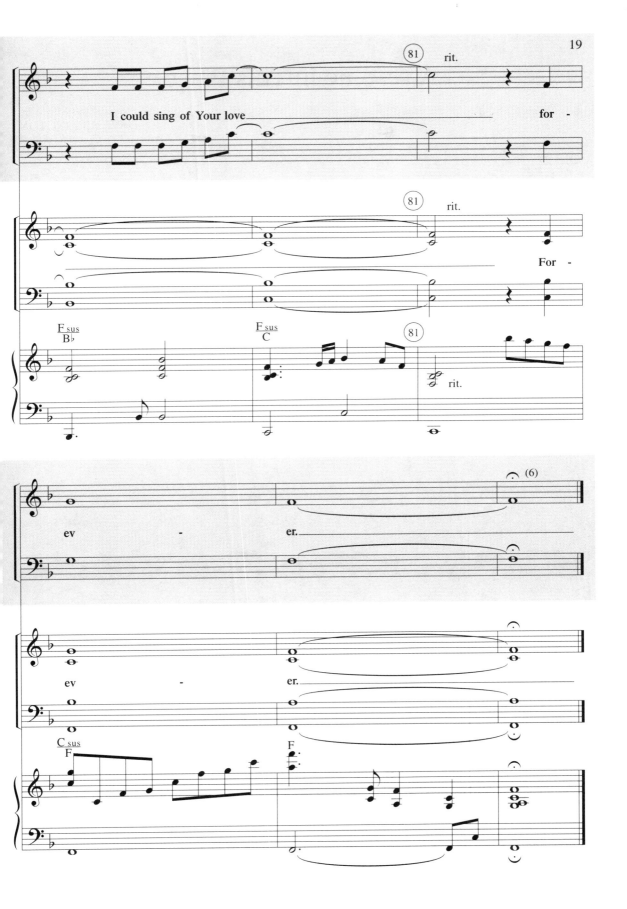

Awesome in This Place

Words and Music by
DAVE BILLINGTON
Arranged by Camp Kirkland

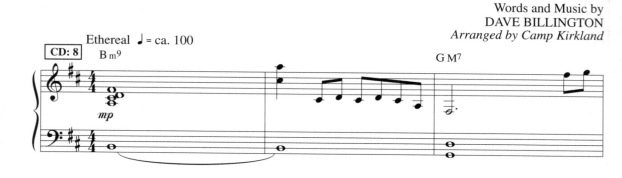

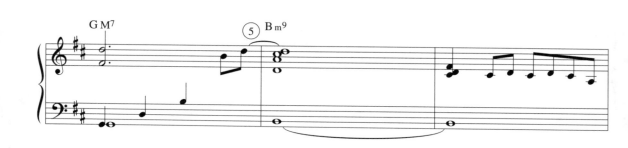

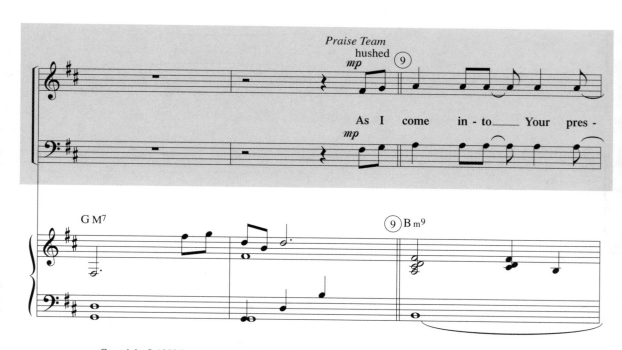

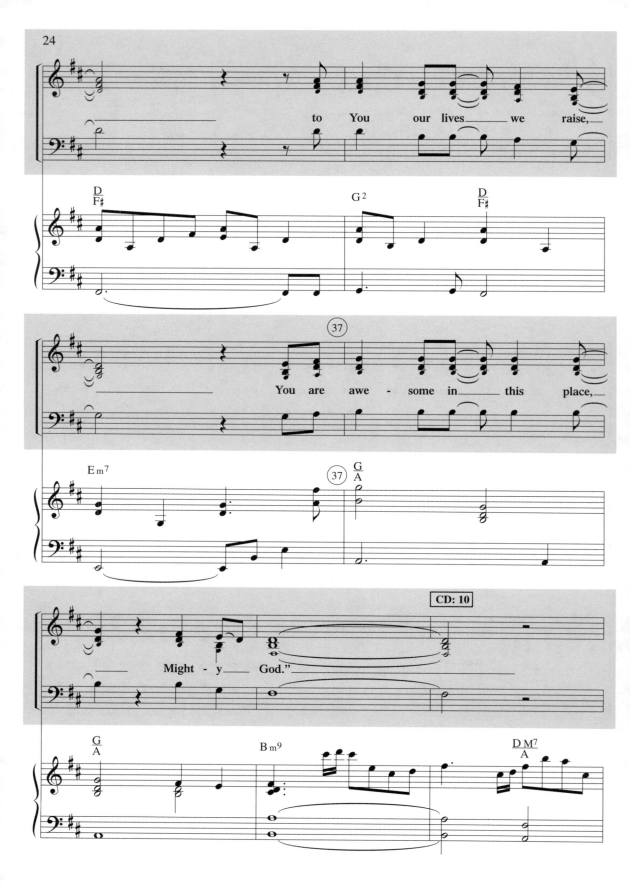

CD: 10

26

to Your sanc - tu - ar - y_____ till we're

to Your sanc - tu - ar - y_____ till we're

B m9

D M7 / A

stand - ing face_____ to face:_____ I look up-on Your coun-

stand - ing face_____ to face:_____ I look up-on Your coun-

G 2

D / F#

A sus

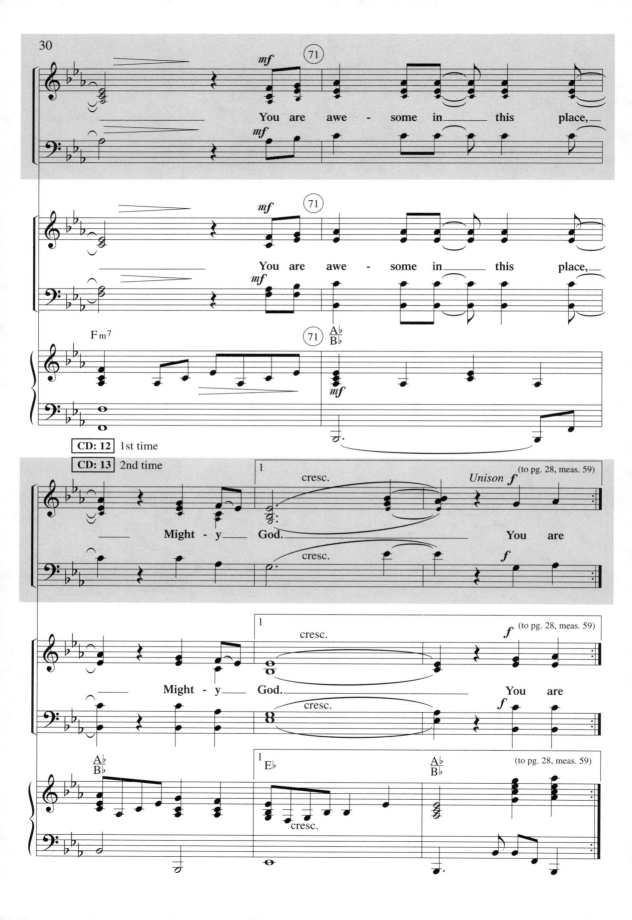

You are awe - some in ____ this place,

You are awe - some in ____ this place,

F m⁷ A♭/B♭

CD: 12 1st time
CD: 13 2nd time

Might - y ____ God. ____ You are

Might - y ____ God. ____ You are

A♭/B♭   E♭   A♭/B♭

cresc.   Unison *f*   (to pg. 28, meas. 59)

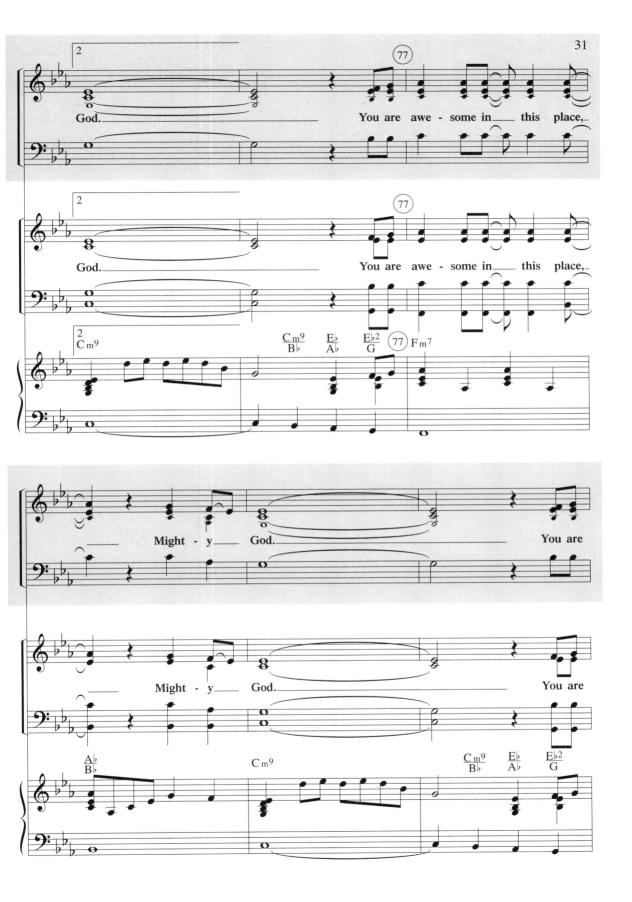

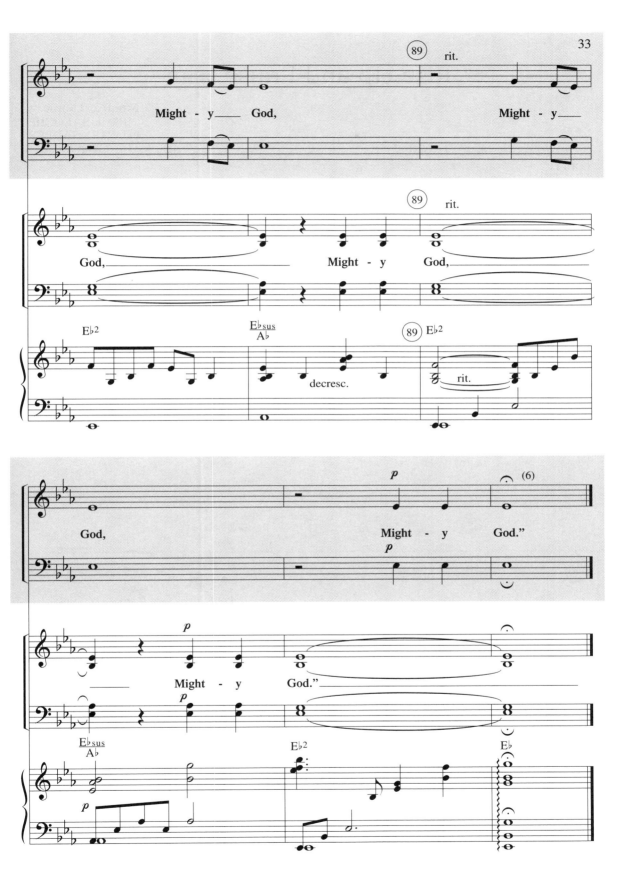

Rise Up and Praise Him

Words and Music by
PAUL BALOCHE
and GARY SADLER
Arranged by Camp Kirkland

With great energy ♩ = ca. 140

CD: 14

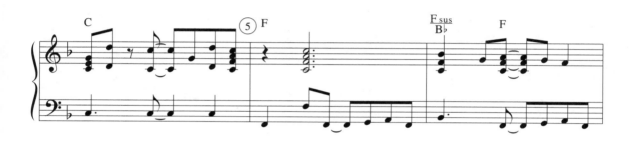

He de - serves____ our____ love;____

He de - serves____ our____ love;____

C   F sus / B♭   F   F sus

28

Rise up____ and praise____ Him,____

28

Rise up____ and praise____ Him,____

28   F   F sus / B♭   C

46

(to pg. 43, meas. 44)

CD: 19

Divisi

Rise up____ and praise____   Rise up____ and praise____

Divisi

D   D   C   G sus/C   G/C   A m/G

Rise up____ and   praise!

Him,____   praise   Him,____

A m/G   G   G sus/C   G

Desire of My Heart

BEVERLY DARNALL

JEFF SLAUGHTER
Arranged by Camp Kirkland

50

would love me so, / could walk this road

And / That

see / bro't

in / me

me / to

a / this

child / mo -

to / ment

call / here

Eb2 / Gb2

⑬

Your / and

own? / now?

All / What -

I'll / ev -

ev - / er

er / you

need / must

is / do,

His

GbM7 / Eb2

wait - / prom -

ing / is -

here / es

for / are

me, / true

Hid - / His

den / love

in / will

the / hold

heart / me

of / up

You / some -

way,

Eb2 / Gb2

CD: 21 1st time
CD: 23 2nd time

a - / some -

lone. / how.

GbM7

52

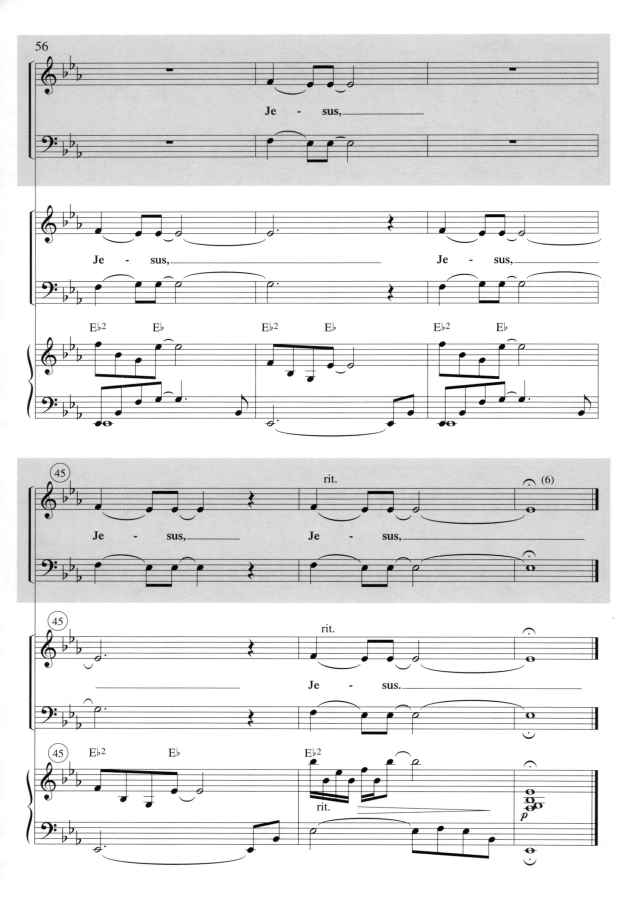

Let Your Love Flow

Words and Music by
DAN ADLER
Arranged by Camp Kirkland

Slowly, soulfully ♩ = ca. 48

CD: 24

Solo

Let Your___

love   flow from me like___ a   foun - tain.___   Let it

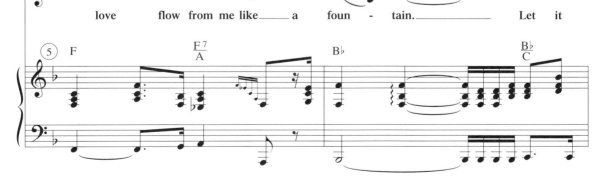

PLEASE NOTE: Copying of this product is NOT covered by CCLI licenses. For CCLI information call 1-800-234-2446.

pour on ev-'ry-one___ I___ see. Dry___

up___ the foun-tain of the sins in me. Let Your

liv - ing wa-ter, let Your liv - ing wa-ter, Let Your

liv - ing wa-ter___ flow so free.

CD: 25

molto rit.

Faster ♩ = ca. 78

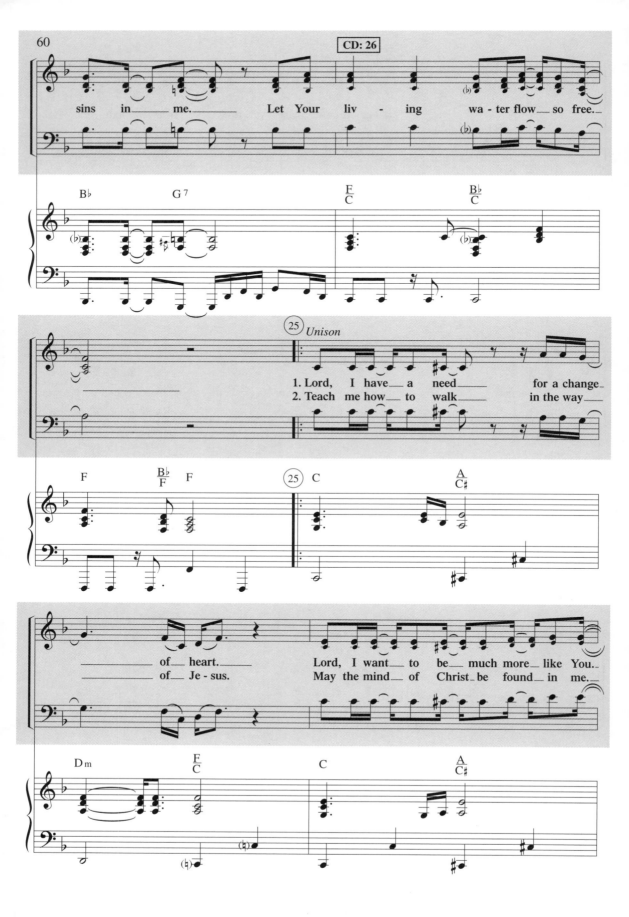

CD: 26

sins in me. Let Your liv - ing wa - ter flow so free.

Bb   G7   F/C   Bb/C

(25) Unison

1. Lord, I have a need for a change
2. Teach me how to walk in the way

F   Bb/F F   (25) C   A/C#

of heart.
of Je - sus.

Lord, I want to be much more like You.
May the mind of Christ be found in me.

Dm   F/C   C   A/C#

(to pg. 60, meas. 25)

CD: 30

*Repeat as many times as desired

*Trax do not repeat

66

68

72

Give Thanks

Words and Music by
HENRY SMITH
Arranged by Camp Kirkland

74

done _____ for __ us. Give thanks! _____

has done for __ us.

Give __ thanks! _____

80

82

84

Open the Eyes of Our Hearts

Words and Music by
DAN ADLER
Arranged by Camp Kirkland

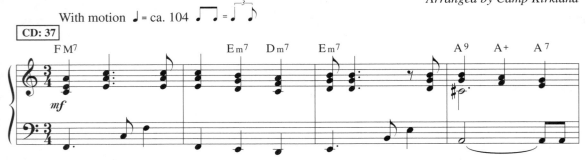

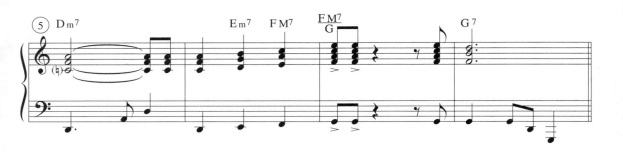

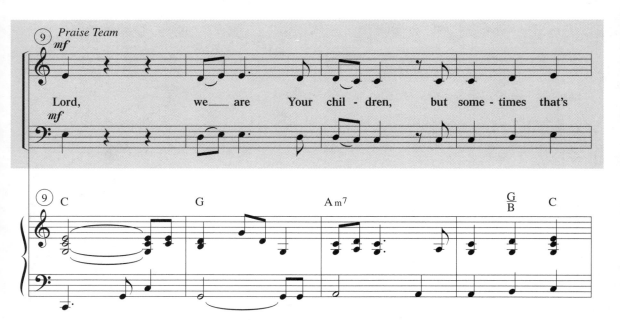

Lord, we＿ are Your chil - dren, but some - times that's

94

There Is No God like You

Words and Music by
DAN WHITTEMORE
Arranged by Camp Kirkland

all a - way._____ You paid a debt that I could

not re - pay;_____ There is no God___ like You._____ O___

(to pg. 97, meas. 5)

be set free.___ I want to be in Christ___ all that

I can be,___ There is no God___ like You.___

There is no God___ like You.___ O___

CD: 47

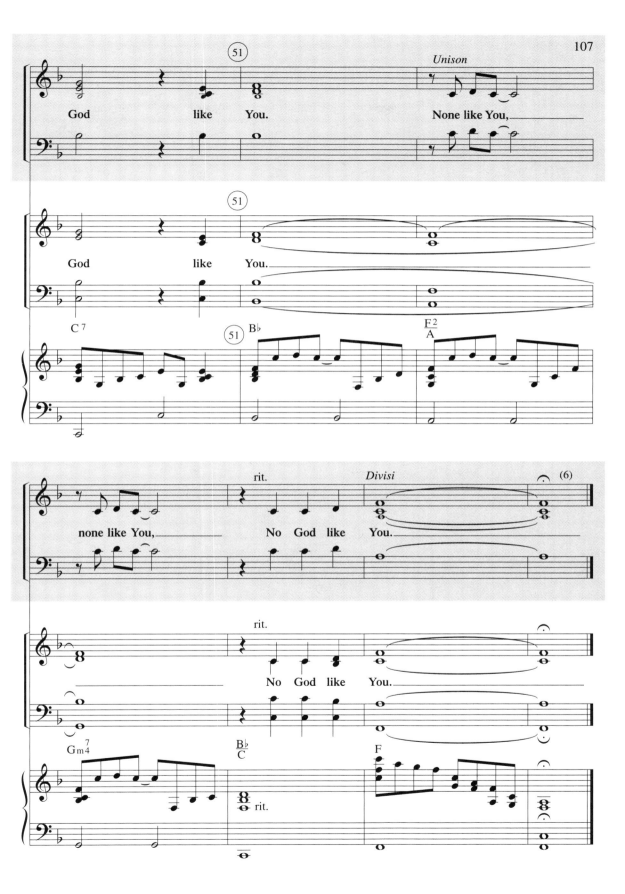

Victory Chant

Words and Music by
JOSEPH VOGELS
Arranged by Camp Kirkland

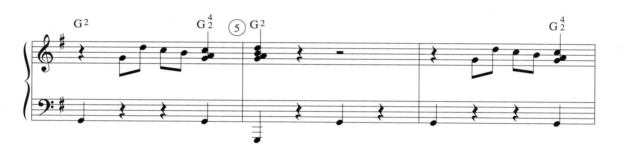

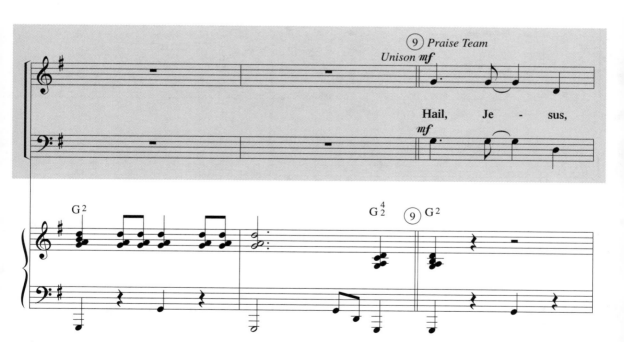

112

king - dom come.

I want to see___ Your king - dom come.

G 2   G sus   G 2   G sus

CD: 50

Not my will but Yours be done._____

Not my will but

G 2   G sus   G 2

O and pro-claim that Je-sus reigns.

in Your name.

Hail, hail,

And pro-claim that Je-sus reigns.

Lion of Ju - dah.

Hail, hail, Lion of Ju - dah.

How pow - er - ful You are.

How pow - er -

CD: 52

124

Step by Step

with

Lead Me

Words and Music by
DAVID STRASSER
Arranged by Camp Kirkland

130

132

134

CD: 58

You're the

Your ways are per-fect, so lead me to-day.

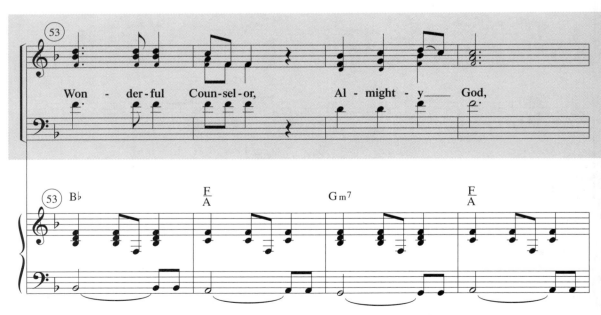

Won - der - ful Coun-sel - or, Al - might - y God,

138

All I Need Is You

Words and Music by
DAN ADLER
Arranged by Camp Kirkland

PLEASE NOTE: Copying of this product is NOT covered by CCLI licenses. For CCLI information call 1-800-234-2446.

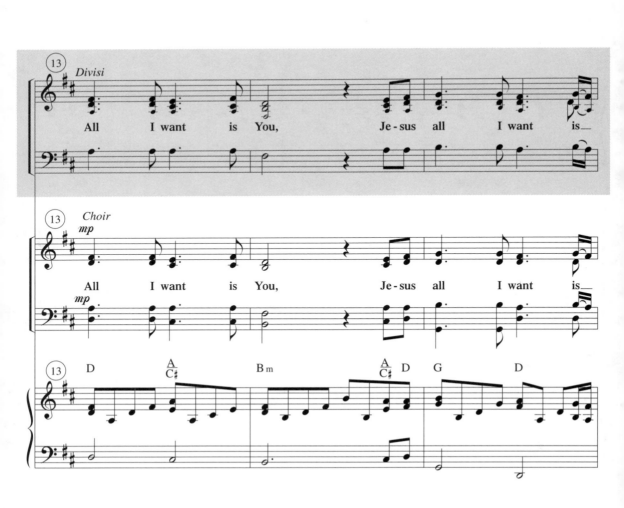

141

144

Come, Now Is the Time to Worship

Words and Music by
BRIAN DOERKSEN
Arranged by Camp Kirkland

for those _____ who glad - ly choose _____ you now. _____

CD: 67

Come,

Come,

Choir
Divisi *mf*

Come,
Divisi *mf*

149

150

for those ___ who glad - ly choose ___ you now.

for those ___ who glad - ly choose ___ you now.

Cm   B♭/C   Cm   Fm7

1 (to pg. 154, meas. 74)   2 CD: 70

1 (to pg. 154, meas. 74)   2

1 B♭ (to pg. 154, meas. 74)   2 B♭

158